# Sweet Malida

# Praise for *Sweet Malida*:

When people say they are "hybrids," it is usually a concoction. With Zilka Joseph, her hybridity is her essence. Zilka, a respected and acknowledged writer and poet, is both Indian and Jewish, a member of the wonderful Bene Israel community of Maharashtra, with whom I had the privilege to live for three years and to remain in contact throughout my life. Zilka Joseph's poems are so authentic, reflecting the Bene Israel community I once knew.

Zilka's ancestors were originally oilpressers in the Konkan villages, but for several generations they have held prestigious positions in Bengal, Gujarat and today's Pakistan. Zilka herself was born in Mumbai, moved to Kolkata with her parents, the marine engineer Solomon (Sunny) Aaron Joseph and his wife Ruby (nee Benjamin), and only in her thirties did she move with her husband to the United States of America. Significantly, they did not migrate, like most of their fellow Bene Israel, to the State of Israel. Therefore, Zilka's trajectory is different from that of many of her coreligionists, and her horizons are broader. Zilka Joseph has been influenced by British colonialism, Indian tradition and American neo-liberalism. In previous books, she struggled with global concepts: displacement, immigration, grief, feminism and oppression, even touching upon human rights. Now *Sweet Malida* is a retreat to childhood memories, albeit continued in new settings, but reminiscent of the beauty of Indian Jewish life in the domestic and communal spheres.

*Sweet Malida* is a delicious read. It is full of the flavours of India, the smells of the spices and the savouriness of unique Bene Israel dishes prepared for Jewish festivals and consumed with relish. Zilka Joseph knows first-hand the shape, the consistency and the tastes of laadus, chana, sharbath, halwa, and fried puris, and the zing of masala, coriander and turmeric, all set against a backdrop of belief in Eliyahoo Hannabi, Elijah the Prophet, in whom Bene Israel devoutly believe, and the ultimate monotheistic God, so inappropriate in an Indian world of many gods.

Zilka Joseph thus embodies hybridity, haunted by Indian delicacies yet encompassed by modernism and impulse. She manages to convey this complexity to her readers with elegance, style, and soul.

—Prof. Shalva Weil is Senior Researcher at the Hebrew University of Jerusalem, Israel. She is editor of several books on India's Jews, including *India's Jewish Heritage* (Marg, 2002), *Indo-Judaic Studies in the Twenty-First Century* (with Nathan Katz et al—Palgrave-Macmillan, 2007), *Karmic Passages* (with David Shulman—OUP, 2008), *Baghdadi Jews in India* (Routledge, 2019), and *The Jews of Goa* (Primus, 2020). She has published over 100 articles, chapters in books, and encyclopedia entries on different aspects of Jews and Judaism in India. In 2021, she was invited to research the Sassoons as Visiting Scholar at the Centre for Financial History at Darwin College, University of Cambridge, UK. In 2022, she was appointed a Fellow of the Royal Historical Society of Great Britain.

***

In an era of globalization that encourages homogeneity, Zilka Joseph's *Sweet Malida* is a timely reminder of the importance of preserving one's unique identity. For displaced communities everywhere, survival takes precedence as they reinvent themselves to gain acceptance in unfamiliar lands—often at the cost of losing sight of their roots. In these evocative and skillfully crafted poems, Zilka reclaims the legacy of the dwindling Bene Israel Jewish community through its culture, cuisine, customs, and her own personal journeys. In doing so, she pushes back against the prejudice that stains societies across the globe and celebrates the fact that it is possible to live in harmony with other communities even while safeguarding one's own rich heritage. Like Draksha-cha Sharbath, these poems offer sweetness on the tongue.

—Menka Shivdasani, author of four poetry collections, co-translator of a Sindhi Partition poetry anthology, has edited anthologies for the American e-zine *www.bigbridge.org*, and *SPARROW*. Her awards include the Ethos Literary Award & WE Eunice de Souza Award. In 1986, she co-founded Poetry Circle, and is Co-Chair, Asia Pacific Writers and Translators. *https://menkashivdasani.in/*

***

The history of a people must be told through a cultural lens and art as much as through a historical narrative of events. I loved the way in which Zilka Joseph, in her latest book, beckons the reader into the world of the Bene Israel, the largest of India's Jewish communities, in Mumbai, where the author was born, and in Kolkata, where she grew up. The introduction and interspersed prose segments and poems illuminate the unique history, culture, and identity of this community, as well as her own journeys as a woman, as an Indian, and as a Jew. She paints an intimate portrait of the Bene Israel as a collective, while still making each poem intensely personal and individualistic. Poems about the prophet Elijah, of special importance to the Bene Israel, such as "Eliyahoo Hanabi" and "Sweet Malida," from which the collection takes its name, are juxtaposed with quotes from the Bible. In these poems the ancestral practices and food ceremonies relating to Elijah are vividly described.

Food is culture. Her charming poems about the preparation of traditional Bene Israel dishes, especially for holidays and the Sabbath, give tangible form to her emotional, philosophical, and cultural musings. One can almost smell and taste the foods, as described in many of the poems, such as "Kaulee Haddi," "Pantoum for Chik-cha Halwa," "A Chirota for my Thoughts," and "Green Kaanji and Destiny," as well as in the prose piece, "The Laadu Makers". Embedded in them are nuanced insights into the personalities of the women who prepared these dishes and of Joseph as a small child. From "Pantoum for Chik-cha Halwa":

*so very different from sweets of home*
*sugar coconut milk colored pink thickening*
*those lost in the deluge shipwrecked*
*would their spirits whisper old recipes*

*sugar rose-tinted coconut milk thickening*
*tired arms bated breath silky cubes cooling*
*do spirits whisper old recipes*
*in a new land new life new history*

Other poems, such as the compelling "Leaf Boat," are more complex in form and rich with sea imagery. It begins:
*In the delta of the east unwieldly Kolkata*
*my flesh clay and flowers and thorns*
*Hooghly my river with ilish come to spawn*

*my body a leaf-boat lamp floated on water*

*the majhis' nets drag, drown in silt*
*the pre-monsoon boar tide rips upstream*
*a dead bull's head, marigolds, lurch in the backwash*

*at Khidderpur docks ships shook in their moorings*

"Man hu? Man hu?", about the Exodus, expands the vista to general Jewish history and displays Joseph's observations of nature, which permeate her previous books. The excellent relationships between the Bene Israel and the other religious communities of India, and to some extent the cultural assimilation of the Indian Jews, come through in poems such as "The Angels of Konkan" and "Mumbai Goddesses."

Remarkably, Joseph, in this collection of poems and short prose pieces, provides the reader with a rich, multilayered portrait of the Bene Israel—and of herself .

—Dr. Joan Roland is Professor Emerita and long-time chair of the History Department at Pace University in New York City. Author of *The Jewish Communities of India: Identity in a Colonial Era,* she has been doing research on the Jews of India for over 40 years.

***

In this deeply moving collection, Zilka Joseph takes us on a journey through memories scented with cumin and cardamom, grief and regret, as her Bene Israel heritage comes alive. Born in Mumbai and having immigrated to the United States as an adult leaving parents and other family behind, Joseph's precise and passionate descriptions transcend time and space, bringing us chironji dough which "fluffed up miraculously/ as it rose up singing/ out of hot oil," and Sabbath tea lights against the backdrop of a Michigan sunset, with her long-gone mother and father standing at her dining table as she "[raises her] palm in prayer,/ [says] the words/ they taught [her] to say.

—Nancy Naomi Carlson, author of *Piano in the Dark*, an Editor's Choice for Poetry Daily, Winner of the 2022 Oxford-Weidenfeld Translation Prize, Co-translator of Wendy Guerra's *DELICATES* (Seagull Books, 2023), noted in *The New York Times*, and Translations Editor, *On the Seawall.*

***

*Sweet Malida* by Zilka Joseph is a collection of nineteen well-crafted poems subtitled "Memories of a Bene Israel Woman." I was struck by the way she connects, in the introduction, a thunderstorm in which her car was nearly washed off the road with thoughts of her father, who was a marine engineer and sailed the stormy seas, and her ancestors' journey from the Middle East to India. Describing the legend of their arrival, she explains how they settled in the village off the Konkan coast of India. More importantly the poems bear witness to the influence of both her parents, whose memories she wants to "bring to life again." The book is devoted exclusively to her Indian-Jewish roots, its customs and traditions, food and culture. The centrality of the prophet Elijah is emphasized in the poem "Eliyahoo Hanabi" and "Sweet Malida" where the celebration of the Malida ceremony, unique to the Bene Israel Jewish people, is narrated. The book is special to me since, as a Bene Israeli poet myself, celebrating many of the customs and traditions in my own poetry and writing, our shared heritage enables me to relate closely to the material in the book. For others not acquainted with the Bene Israel Jews of India, the book will be an interesting and valuable document in verse, of both personal and historical value. Zilka is an award winning poet.

—Kavita Ezekiel Mendonca, author of *Family Sunday and Other Poems* and *Light of The Sabbath*

***

Zilka's poems are an invitation into the Bene Israel kitchen of her youth. Come sit at the table as her mother and her grandmother spice their dishes with history, nostalgia, and longing that will leave you hungry for more. A hybrid of form and structure takes the reader from the origin story of the Bene Israel to the origin story of Zilka herself. Each poem is a taste of turmeric, coconut, coriander, and chili, sweet, but also savory, heavy with memory. "Who knew heaven could be like this."

—Erica Lyons, National Jewish Book Awards finalist, Founder of *Asian Jewish Life*, Chair of the Hong Kong Jewish Historical Society, and author of several children's books titles including *Zhen Yu and the Snake, Counting on Naamah,* and the forthcoming *On a Chariot of Fire.*

***

Zilka Joseph's *Sweet Malida* is an important book for anyone with a taste for poetry and interest in the micro-minorities of India, specifically the Jews. Indian Jewry is represented by seven groups that can be broadly divided into old and new Jews. The old Jews comprise the communities of the Bene Israel of Maharashtra, the Cochini of Kerala, and the Baghdadi of Mumbai and Kolkata. While the Bene Israel and the Cochini have been resident in India for several centuries, perhaps more than a millennium, the Baghdadis settled in India primarily in the late 18th and the early 19th centuries. The new Jews belong to the several Judaizing movements that emerged in India since the mid-20th century, viz., the Bene Menashe of Manipur and Mizoram, the Bene Ephraim and the Noachides of Andhra Pradesh, and a section of a Christian congregation of the Chettiars of District Erode, Tamil Nadu that has started practising Judaism.

Jews form the smallest religious minority of India, with their population estimated to be in the range of five thousand. In spite of their numerical insignificance they have produced several writers and poets—disproportionately more than their small numbers warranted, with women particularly prominent, including Esther David, Sophie Judah, Meera Mahadevan (nee Miriam Aaron Jacob Mendrekar), Sheela Rohekar, Jael Silliman, Ruby Daniel, Kavita Ezekiel Mendonca, Carmit Delman, Angelica Jacob, Sheba Jeremiah Nagaokar, Sadia Shepard, etc. They have published both prose and poetry in several languages, primarily English and Hindi. The best known of the Indian Jewish poets has been Nissim Ezekiel, who came to be acknowledged as the father of India's modern English poetry. His Jewishness figures prominently in many of his poems and also those of his daughter Kavita Ezekiel Mendoca, but their Bene Israel community never emerged as the focus of any of their poetry collections, unlike Zilka Joseph's *Sweet Malida*. It is this that distinguishes this collection and makes it highly significant. It is poetry where the poet's soul lies bare. And if that poetry captures the feeling and experience of belonging to a micro-minority, then it emerges as an invaluable source for anyone with a genuine interest in that community. As Nissim Ezekiel famously wrote:

*A poem is an episode,*
*Completed in an hour or two,*
*But poetry is something more.*
*It is the why, the how, the what, the flow.*
*From which a poem comes.*

—Dr. Navras J. Aafreedi, Ph.D., author of *Jews, Judaizing Movements and the Traditions of Israelite Descent in South Asia*. Assistant Professor, Department of History, Presidency University, Research Fellow, Institute for the Study of Global Antisemitism and Policy (ISGAP), New York, and Salzburg Global Fellow.

# Dedication

*For my ancestors*

*In memory of my parents Ruby and Sunny (Solomon) Joseph*

*With gratitude to Benjamin J. Israel, historian, scholar and author*

*In tribute to the great Bene Israel poet, Nissim Ezekiel*

*Always, for John*

# Sweet Malida

## Memories of a Bene Israel Woman

### by Zilka Joseph

Foreword by Jerry Pinto

Mayapple Press
Pippa Rann Books & Media

2024

North American Edition ISBN 978-1-952781-19-3
Library of Congress Control Number: 2023947326
International Edition ISBN 978-1-913738-20-4
Printed in India by Replika Press Pvt. Ltd.

**Acknowledgements:**
Thanks to the editors of the journals and books that published these poems,
some in different versions: *Paper Brigade Daily; 101 Jewish Poems for the Third
Millennium* (Ashland Poetry Press, Ashland, Ohio, 2021); *Cha, Journal of Asian
Arts; Joao-Roque Literary Journal; Rattle; RASA,* an imprint of *Whetstone Magazine;
Poetry at Sangam.* "Kaulee Haddi" and "Homegrown" were published in my
chapbook *Lands I Live In* (Mayapple Press, Woodstock, NY, 2007). "Voyage" and
"Whose Voices Were Heard" were published in *In Our Beautiful Bones* (Mayapple
Press, 2021).

**Gratitude:**
   My deepest gratitude to Mayapple Press, and to the editor, Judith Kerman
for believing in my work since she published my very first book in 2007. Also
to Jerry Pinto for his generosity and kindness, and to Prabhu Guptara of Pippa
Rann Books, UK, for publishing this international edition.

   Thanks to Rowe Lee-Mills and the Crawford Lee-Mills Fund, to Sharon
Backstrom and to late Nancy Williams, who support my work.

   To artist and shamanic practitioner Raina (nee Ezekiel) Imig for the fabulous
paintings you created for my book cover, and for your generosity.

   To acclaimed scholars who have done groundbreaking research on the Jews
of India— Drs. Joan Roland, Shalva Weil, and Navras Aafreedi, my humble
thanks.

   To Menka Shivdasani, Kavita Ezekiel Mendonca, Nancy Naomi Carlson, and
Erica Cohen Lyons, exceptional poets, writers, translators, whose works light up
this world, for your graciousness and support, I am truly grateful.

   Thanks to John, for being my partner on this long journey.

Book and cover design and layout by Judith Kerman. Cover art, details from
"Malida with Blue Bowl" and "Elijah with Fiery Chariot," © Raina Imig 2023,
acrylic on canvas. Photo of author by John Joseph. Typeset in Calisto MT, with
cover title in Nova Cut.

# Contents

# Foreword:

## On food, on poetry, on Zilka Joseph

Last year, when I was writing a column for *The Hindustan Times* on walking my city, I ended up on its outskirts in Panvel where a Jain architect married to a Muslim poet and architect took me to a Jewish synagogue where I completed my trio of malidas. The first malido I had eaten was at the house of a Parsi friend; then a Bohri invited me and I was introduced to another kind of malida. And then at Panvel, I had a Jewish malida, which does not form part of the cuisine of any Indian Jewish group as far as I know, except for the oldest of them, the Bene Israeli. Each of these dishes was different, each delicious in its own way, and some element of this deliciousness was the difference, the way in which tongue and palate and throat received the benison of food. I will not belabour the metaphor but I will say that my country is, I believe, built around the notion of difference.

*Sweet Malida* by Zilka Joseph got me thinking about the role of food in poetry; how does that sensual-sensuous-sensory experience work in the world of words that are pushing against and past meaning to create a new awareness of the richesse of human experience? We know food is our common heritage; we know food is not innocent, not since the fruit of knowledge was eaten in the Garden, not since Persephone ate a few pomegranate seeds, and certainly not on the subcontinent where the role of the divinity seems to have been reduced to that of a dietician. But, for the exile, for the émigré, for the expat, for the migrant, food is an anchor. It holds and it binds. The chain is crusted by barnacles of experience, the line is thinned by the new and by the demands of integration. But it is tenacious, it will remain, and it will trip us up when least expected. In Joseph's careful hands, food resists the blandishments of nostalgia, the cryptocurrency of memory banks. 'I sing of the wilderness within,' she writes in her collection *What Dread* and this wilderness is as much body as it is spirit.

Certainly, food acts as metaphor for her but then you might argue that every word is a metaphor wherever deployed. So, we begin again. Food is what you experience when you eat. What you experience is determined by who you are at that point. The child who hates papaya grows up to love it. The adolescent who sneers at olives finds them perfect in his forties, paired with the cheese he once called stinky. Malida is malida until it is not; when it is not, it is because it is now mnemonic, it is now portent, it is symbol. Just as drakshacha sharbat is drakshacha sharbat until you find yourself having to take on the role of a grandmother, or of a mother when, like Ruth, you find yourself standing amid alien corn.

Here it is again, the juxtaposition of food and thought, food and people, food and othering. This is from a poem 'Introduction to Circles' from another collection, *Lands I Live In*. The persona the poet chooses to speak from here is an initiate into the mysteries of book clubs in the US.

> *I find it hard to answer, eat and while eating talk*
> *about the caste system, the status of women—*
> *or the lack of it, terrified of dropping crumbs*
> *of spilling my wine, all the while*
> *explaining behavioural patterns and traditions*
> *of life forms on my planet.*

There is a simultaneity here that we often forget in our valorisation of food. That it can be a source of social lubrication—I imagine petits fours and tiny sandwiches, both carefully curated, both liable to disintegrate into crumbs at Martha's book club. Food can also be a signal of the intentions of all present—I cannot attack you if my hands are full of food—although we all know now that dinner-time hostilities are a time-honoured tradition both within families and without. Food can be sin and it can be solace. So much like poetry, so much like Joseph's poetry.

*Sweet Malida* is a rare treat; it lets us into the home of a Jewish family in India. It allows us glimpses of the family's history, taking us across three continents and a variety of time zones. It pokes gentle fun at genetic determinism and pays homage to the tradition of kosher, kept by a community that had forgotten the word but kept the spirit alive. Would that we could all remember the spirit of the Word, whichever word it is, and not get caught in legalities.

In that Joseph reminds us how often food becomes central to the notion of community, both in terms of the flesh and the feeling. Malida takes its place with the prasadam, with the Communion Host, with the dates and salt of the iftar with which the faithful break roza. This is a rare book, springing linguistic surprises and ranging wide and free, from the ravens who fed the Prophet Elijah to the ilish that brightens the eye of the Bengali.

This is how we lived, all of us, with formica tabletops and hand-knitted tokens of love from grandmothers. This is how we are, all of us, exiles from the Land of Childhood where Santa Claus might visit a Jewish home. This is how we want to be and this is how we shall be, for always we will have this memory:

*My beloveds are with me.*
*That is blessing enough.*


Jerry Pinto

Mumbai, May 2024, the month of the gold of mangoes
and the night of jamun, of ice apple gelidity and searing heat

And may God grant you the dew of Heaven and of the riches of the land and an abundance of grain and wine.

—The Blessing of Heaven and Earth, *Genesis* 27:28

The song of my experience sung,
I knew that all was yet to sing.
My ancestors, among castes,
Were aliens crushing seed for bread.

—From "Background, Casually" by Nissim Ezekiel

*And it shall be, that thou shalt drink of the brook; and I have commanded the ravens to feed thee there. So he went and did according unto the word of the Lord: for he went and dwelt by the brook Cherith, that is before Jordan.*

*And the ravens brought him bread and flesh in the morning, and bread and flesh in the evening; and he drank of the brook.*

—About Prophet Elijah. *1 Kings* 17:2-6

*He himself went a day's journey into the wilderness, and came and sat down under a juniper tree: and he requested for himself that he might die; and said, It is enough; now, O Lord, take away my life; for I am not better than my fathers.*

*And as he lay and slept under a juniper tree, behold, then an angel touched him, and said unto him, Arise and eat.*

*And he looked, and, behold, there was a cake baken on the coals, and a cruse of water at his head.*

—About Prophet Elijah. *1 Kings* 19:4-10

# What's in My Bones

I was born in Mumbai and grew up in Kolkata, India, part of a community called the Bene Israel, which is the oldest Jewish community in India.

My ancestors were called *Shanwar telis*—Saturday Oil Pressers, (*tel* is the Marathi word for oil, *teli*, one who presses seeds for oil)— as that was the profession many took up. Since they did not work on *shanwar*—Saturday, the Sabbath, they were called *Shanwar tellis*. Many theories about their origins exist.

One theory of their arrival is that two ships from the Middle East were shipwrecked on the west coast of India in 175 B.C.E. The survivors settled in villages and made a new life for themselves. Some say that seven men, or perhaps seven couples, survived. Others think they came after the destruction of the Second Temple in 70 C.E., or that they were descendants of the Lost Tribes who came around the tenth century, perhaps around King Solomon's reign. The most popular theory is that they were fleeing the rule of the Greek overlord Epiphanes in 175 B.C.E. However, still other scholars think that they came from Yemen, Persia, or South Arabia in the fifth or sixth century C.E.

The new arrivals, who had lost everything, were peacefully allowed to settle and travel. They adopted Indian ways, clothes, foods, and kept the Sabbath. Except for the Shema and maybe a few other prayers, they did not remember most rituals. When Christian missionaries discovered this community, they found that these people did not know of the existence of Hanukkah. This supports the theory that they arrived before the second century. In India, they were not persecuted, and it became their home. Their descendants thrived, and they have become active and successful every profession, including literature, art, music dance, science, social work, Hollywood and Bollywood, and the military.

"Voyage" is the opening poem of my book *In Our Beautiful Bones.* The epigraph refers to the Upanishads, the ear being a vessel for divine messages. I describe a thunderstorm in which my car was nearly washed off the road. A bolt of lightning hit somewhere close by, followed by a deafening clap of thunder. Paralyzed by terror for a few moments, I felt lifted out of my body and suspended in some other world or dimension. Then, suddenly, I was back. At that moment, I thought of my father, who was a marine engineer in

Bombay, and who had sailed for decades, from the days of the steam ship to when Diesel vessels became common. The storms he had weathered on the high seas connected me with him in a strange new way, as if some secret knowledge had been transferred to me. At the same time, I felt connected to my ancestors' journey from somewhere in the Middle East to India.

*...the bow*
*of my ship rose*
*to meet the horizon,*

*and my father, the Chief,*
*roared to his engineers,*
*their faces streaked with oil*

*and boiler suits sweat drenched;*
*men whose torn lips*
*bled as another peal shook*

*the flailing vessel, and we turned*
*our faces to the upper*
*deck. Like our Jewish*

*ancestors wrecked on the*
*Konkan coast thousands*
*of years ago, we waited*

*but no calm came*
*until the wind suddenly*
*fell.*

Growing up in my culturally-complex family, I devoured world epics, folktales, literatures, mythology, and because India was colonized for 200 years by the British, I was influenced by their literature as well, and by American culture, particularly music and film. Animals, wildlife, fish, birds, Nature, also became important to me.

I migrated to the US with my husband when we were in our mid-thirties, leaving behind in Kolkata my larger-than-life father, Solomon (Sunny) Aaron Joseph, and my quiet and wise mother Ruby. I bring my parents to life again in my poems, which reflect a unique blend of cultures and ideas, and which trace my own growth, my journeys—personal, geographical, spiritual—my hardships and triumphs.

Life in a new land is never easy. We have to educate, break barriers, and fight to be heard:

*this is your ancestors' ark*
*rise rise up singing*
. . .

*can you see us dancing in the dark and in the rain*
*and in the moonlight the firelight the lamplight*

*dancing in the sun*
 *in our own shining skin*
 *in our beautiful bones*

# Eliyahoo Hanabi

*—the Malida ceremony of the Bene Israel*

Give thanks to the Prophet Elijah!
Eliyahoo hanabi!
Eliyahoo hanabi!

Let us heap the sugar-sprinkled poha
tall as a pyramid, mixed with shredded
coconut, precious dried fruit and nuts,
scented with the most fragrant
of spices. O Elijah, can you taste

the nutmeg, the cardamom, the freshly
sliced mangoes, guava, chikoo, apples and
bananas arranged like garlands? Can you see
the pomegranate seeds dotting the top
of the rice, bursting sweet juice
and tartness? Can you smell

the red rose petals
scattered everywhere,
the cups of cloves?
Accept our thanks!

Let us say barakha over
each item, ha'etz, ha'adama.
The fruits that grow on trees of hard
wood, the fruits that grow on soft
trunks of fiber. Phool-chi barakha,
praise the flowers that give us so much
pleasure. Join us! Descend in your fiery

chariot, where it ascended once, as it left
a cleft in the rock in Sagav village, where
pilgrims come to Alibaug, the soil
our wandering ancestors were
blown onto by the storm. They reached
land, survived. Feast

with us, we humbly ask, O granter
of wishes, as we chant
our gratitude, our prayer—
words of Malida-chi barakha
circle our offerings, rise up

to meet you in the clouds,
touch your flaming chariot
your horses of fire.

Eliyahoo hanabi!
Eliyahoo hanabi!

# Sweet Malida

Sweet malida,
a mix of water-softened
flattened rice, sugar,
dried fruits and nuts,
was a dish made

for Shabbath, or for breaking
our fasts. Cooling, light
on the palate, and
to the body and the spirit,
it was welcome in the heat
of day or night. We had many foods
in common with our Muslim,
Christian and Hindu neighbors,
and we often celebrated together
their festivals or ours. I relished

particularly fresh coconut,
the regional staple, its milk
or its flesh added to almost
every dish. But this was to me
the best way to eat it;
finely grated
by my mother's hands,

left unsweetened
and sprinkled haphazardly
on the malida, juicy threads
with a fleck of stubborn
brown kernel here and there
that sometimes crunched
in your teeth like sand,
and you winced and swallowed it,

knowing that there was no
simpler or purer
or truer form than that.

# The Angels of Konkan

*—Navgaon, Maharashtra, is where, it is believed, the ancestors of the Bene Israel were shipwrecked, and where a ruined cemetery exists today.*

From tumbled sands and shattered bark
blurred shadows dragged us

                    (where were we)
                    they dried our battered bodies

bound our wounds
clothed us in woven cotton

                    fed us warm food (that we could not
                    name then) with their hands

and as Elijah ate of bread and flesh
the ravens gave him so also we ate

                    and drank of the cool water brought
                    from brooks (who were these healers)

then in fields of grass near the sea
we buried our dead— the ones we found

                    (where are they now)
                    set gravestones to remember

they let us pray as we wished
and giving thanks to Adonai

                    learned the craft of oil pressers
                    (did our tribe know it already)

ate what our laws permitted
and praising this vast green land

                    its rich soil its rivers its ghats
                    its grains its fish and fowl

we blessed the hearts
the living hands

                  of the villagers
                  who saved us

# Choral Sonnet

We knew the Shema, kept Shabbath, diet
rules, performed circumcision on our sons,
observed Passover. We lived in our own
world, thrived. Christians discovered us. Later

they taught us Hebrew, translated holy
books to Marathi, educated us,
but could not convert us. *Lost Tribes?*—folks said,
some laughed, *impure*. Even among us we

separated "dark" from "fair." From Kochi
came Rahabi, who sent us three scholars.
Torah, rituals, rules, we absorbed daily.
Did we need anything to define us?

Let the world scoff at the Cohanim gene
found in our blood. We always knew the truth.

# Not One Fish

*—David Rahabi is a central figure in many stories, including one saying that he came in 1000 CE. He may actually have been David Ezekiel Rahabi (1694-1772) from Cochin on the Malabar Coast, south of Konkan, who helped to revive Judaism among the Bene Israel.*

So David Rahabi of Malabar traveled north up the west coast and encountered the shanwar telis, who had taken the names of the villages for their own. He wondered at the oil pressers and farmers, others who made a living by other rural professions, these women and men who had lived as a caste among the locals. So long unknown, this mysterious community, so apart from the urban world. They did not call themselves Jews, nor did they know the word. But he was impressed by the ancient rituals they practiced, the powerful prayer they remembered and used for all occasions—the Shema Israel, which had kept them together.

As legend goes, he asked the women to prepare a feast for him from the bounty of the Arabian Sea.

Would they pick crab and shrimp?
Mussel, clam, or bottom feeders?

No.
Not
one
fish.

Not one
fish
without
fins and scales
had they chosen.

Not one fish
without fins
or scales
was served.

They brought him white-fleshed fish like paplet, and oily fish like bangda and tarli, fresh and flavorful, and salty as the waters that brought the Bene Israel hence from the land of Solomon and David.

He knew then: they kept *kosher*,
a word they did not recall,
just kept a simple faith
in the God of Abraham.

# Man hu? Man Hu?

*—"Upon the face of the wilderness there lay a small round thing, as small as the hoar frost on the ground."* Book of Exodus.

Some said manna was the dew,
some said it fell and dried
with the dew, white,
coriander-like seeds
of crystal.

Jewels harvested before sun-up.
A miracle food the sojourners,
led by Moses into the wilderness,
survived on for forty years.

Sweet, some said it was, like wafers
and honey. Some said it was eaten
plain. Some that it was baked
on hot desert stones or made
into bread. Or added to bread.
Some said, like needles
of sea salt, it crumbled. Too fine
to be ground or baked at all.

*Man hu? Man hu?*—
they asked in Aramaic—
what is it? What is it?

Or did the word "man"
mean aphids? In Sinai,
the waxy honeydew of scaly
insects sifts to the ground
from tamarisks like snow.

In Asia Minor, drifting clusters
of lichens, driven by winds, settle
thick and fast on arid lands.

A "form of dew" that "hardens
and assumes the form of a grain,"
was one man's report in 1921.

What was it? What was it
that fed them all?

I imagine a desert city today,
in the hazy cool of dawn,
a flour-like dew sifting
in slow motion,
drops clinging

to leaves,
drying quickly
into brittle beads,

crows and sparrows
frenziedly feasting

before the sun's rays
melt it all away.

# What Ravens Do

It was said when the skies cleared and the waters

retreated,
Noah released
a raven. It circled long and stayed

aloft until the waters dried. (Some muttered it was good,

it was Yahveh's protective spirit).

Then, it flew away.
It did not return.

Was the saturated earth ready? What

carrion did the raven find? Why call

the rough avian who did what the Creator

created it to do, unclean?

Impure?
Evil?

And call only the gentle dove good?

Hail it, with an olive twig in its beak, a symbol of peace?

What other sustenance could the ragged mountain Ararat

upon which Noah's ark came to rest

provide the carnivores he had husbanded

so dutifully
in his hold?
Was it time?

The raven               was the answer.
And still
they called it

vile.                   Foul              scavenger.

Was
it not the
wild ravens

that Elohim         commanded      to deliver bread

and meat, morning     and night,        dawn and dusk

to Elijah


by a brook

                  at the edge

                                  of Jordan?

# Leaf Boat

In the delta of the east unwieldly Kolkata
      my flesh clay and flowers and thorns
            Hooghly, my river, with ilish come to spawn

my body a leaf-boat lamp floated on water

the majhis' nets drag, drown in silt
      the pre-monsoon bore tide rips upstream
            a dead bull's head, marigolds, lurch in the backwash

at Khidderpur docks ships shook in their moorings

***

they moored the ship to trees, Dad told me
      no quays yet in Galveston, and the mosquitoes huge,
            larger than the ones that bit him in Burundi

            the third eye is the unsleeping captain of the dark

            braved thunder fire flood
            slaved in the engine room
            never sleeping when the storm hit
            his commands whip through the darkness

bringing them safe to the other side

***

drive up north to where

Dum Dum airport flashes like a starship
      metal the wings eyes looking down
      wind hot and moist
      the abyss opening

            wave after Atlantic wave my mother weeps

***

                    in Kumartulli
goddesses rise like breath
from river mud in the fingers of artisans
the dhak sounds  Durga wakes it is time
ten days she visits then immersed

melts back into river mud, O mother
how varied our gods our lands our homes
women weep *Ma come back again*

                something breaks somewhere in my brain
I hear her voice two oceans away

                            ***

my man from South India now lives among strangers
                with this gold chain and silk sari he married me

        he calls me to fly to him soon soon soon
                one land our languages separate as oil on water

the map—
braided lines in the palm of my hand

                            ***

somewhere out west it is sunset
                the porthole is a ball of flame
                        I leave the sliced orange untouched on white plate

his heart was captured by the Snow Queen once

I dream
he is standing with a scroll in his hands
            and the ice cliffs inside him are shattering
                    his words are for me the roses too
                    his voice is soft as evening

                            ***

breakfast time
in Park Circus the new Philips pop-up toaster shines

inside it a brown mouse is eating crumbs
        smells of champagne waft in from first class
            clink-clink behind the navy pleated curtain

my father puts a slice of Modern Bread in

the clock strikes one the little mouse leaps into his face
        we laugh so hard we cannot eat
            my arms are oars
                the majhis are singing

***

in the Sunderbans the sun is sinking

mangrove roots like ribs
fields and fields of fiddler crabs

        fishermen light kerosene torches on the deck
        lock themselves in below

the boat rocks and tilts
the hurricane lantern shakes
tiger claws break through wood

the widows' village is full
where are the fishermen then honey-gatherer husbands

        I shall fear no evil in this valley of tides
            we walk through the shadow of the unknown world

my third eye is the unsleeping captain of the dark

***

draw the curtain it is time is it time
        one little mouse did not escape though it tried
            prepare for landing

sometimes mice can turn into birds
     in New York his ship pulled out Dad said
          above the roar of the engines they shouted to him

a girl child

west to east
west to east the planet turns

I was born Thursday in monsoon rain
     night time East coast time
          in Bombay a baby opens her eyes

               ***

throw blades of grass to the wind
which direction, which direction does it blow
     do not move, do not leave
          your seats till the seat belt sign goes off

so young my parents
     feeding pigeons in Trafalgar Square
     how they sailed the world

     Solomon my father king of the engine room
     king of the house king of our destiny

     sweet mother Ruby loving and mild
     more precious to me than jewels
     their daughter prepares to leave

               ***

     next year in Jerusalem Granny prayed

and safe return dear husband from Egypt's trenches
soldiers fall all around him
some of her letters survive but the photos from Palestine
     are gone are gone

     multi-foliate lotuses open to the sun

***

in Bombay how many Shemas did she say
come back Aaron from Britain's war

his limbs collapse with some disease
just thirty-six when his father his uncles
say Kaddish for him

young Hannah in a white sari at his side

***

O Hannah of Bandra

mother of three small sons
and your five year old daughter dead in her grave

Hannah alone
selling all your gold

your journey just beginning

***

fragments

of letters sent to Hannah
in 1917
he drew maps drew diagrams in his own hand

and talked of Cairo and Alexandria the friends he made

where are they now

my third eye is the unsleeping captain of the dark

purple ink turns brown
writing fades

fish swim in murky water
lift the words in their mouths

O carry them safe to the other side

\*\*\*

in my dream
the whales are singing

check the dorsal this is how we identify migrants

in ancient time my ancestors sailed east
it is said

west to east they sailed
west to east

safe journey to the other side

\*\*\*

three ships wrecked on the Konkan coast
what star what moon saved them

who drowned in salt who breathed the sand
who flailed who flew who fell
who swam who dived whose eyes turned
to pearls who sang to the angels of the deep

who lived to ask
the whales the story
of how they were swept to shore

\*\*\*

in my dream
the whales are singing
check the dorsal: this is how we identify migrants

my ancestors once
        a village on the Konkan coast

        the third eye is the unsleeping captain of the dark

look up
        did David's Star keep them alive
        Shabbath lights flicker in villages

the anchor

        is lifting
        oh where to now

        I am so tired I am so tired

see the stars
        are forming strange new words
        a map a compass and you beside me

                my body a leaf boat
                lamp floated on water

# Mumbai Goddesses

We lived in Shivaji Park when I first asked
my parents about Santa—because he brought presents,

and my picture books showed him flying—
in a sleigh drawn by reindeer over fields and mountains of

snow in cold countries where white people lived
in huge houses with fat furniture and funny things

called fireplaces. We did some fun stuff for Rosh Hashana
and Passover but this was different. Like Eid, when our Muslim

friends and neighbors brought biryani and phirni, our Christian ones
brought fruitcake, marzipan and kul-kuls, and went for midnight

mass to lit-up churches in Mahim and Bandra. I was
mesmerized by the big paper stars and colored lights that hung

outside homes and roadside shrines. My friends
always got what they wanted—red bicycles, blonde

blue-eyed dolls, tea-sets, comic books. That summer,
inside a hand-me-down picture book of festivals I found

a life-size (folded) crepe paper Santa, a springy
"accordion" Santa. I stretched and stretched him

hard till he reached his girth and full height,
he grew much taller and bigger than me, and

then climbing up onto the headboard of my bed,
hung him up so his big black boots

would swing somewhere near the top
of my head when I slept. His right leg

was shorter than his left, and would not straighten
but bounced up and down like a yoyo,

his fluffy, yellow-white beard was crooked,
but his face was like an apple, all kind and smiley.

It was a sweltering night, the fans whining overhead,
the mosquitoes fierce. When Granny turned in her sleep

and snored, our shared bed creaked. I tried hard
to keep my eyes and my ears shut. I woke the next

morning, sun glaring in my face. Three gifts
lay on my bed, wrapped in pretty paper!

I pounced, ripped them open, sat in a sea
of torn gift paper, rumpled bedclothes,

mis-matched covers. And Granny sat by me
on the bed,  her silver hair in a plait, Mum

standing close, her long black hair
spilling from her bun, and all of us

stunned by the magic of Santa, his perfect
choice of puzzles, wooden building

blocks, a wildlife coloring book (how did
he know I loved animals?). Their voices rose

and fell like swallows, their eyes darted from me
to the gifts, to the bed, to the paper, to me

again, and to the uneven-legged Santa—who,
tormented  by the mid-May heat, was wilting

to a pale ghost of Long John Silver. He held no
interest for me anymore. My eyes were riveted

to the two women whose hands touched mine.
They looked just like the goddesses

in my picture books—Athena, Freia,
Durga, Gaia, their faces glowing

with a not-of-this-earth radiance.

# My Cup Runneth Over

Draksha-cha Sharbath. Sherbet of raisins. Our cups overflow with this special drink for Shabbath, or to break the fast at Yom Kippur. Fresh wine made from long, black raisins we bought from New Market in Kolkata for these occasions. Instant sugar high for a kid like me, or for adults who had fasted all day. Such sweetness, such satisfaction. And we believed, just like in Keats' "Ode to Autumn," that everything was "conspiring with the sun…to load and bless" us with abundance, and like the wasps, we thought "warm days would never cease."

In Keats' poem, the figure of Autumn watches the winnowing of grain and the pressing of apples as she sits in a field or shed. I, too, was a witness—to the making of our simple sharbath. Hannah, my grandmother, was the real head of the house when I was small. She had been widowed at 36 when her husband—also 36, a doctor and army captain who had served the British on the frontlines in Egypt and Palestine during World War I and who retuned home because he was suffering from what they called "shell shock." He died soon after. Before that they had lost a five-year old girl child to diphtheria.

After her husband's death, Hannah brought up three young sons on a small Government pension, with the help of her highly educated siblings and some money she got by selling her jewelry. Her youngest, my father Solomon the marine engineer, was the son she spent most of her years with. She lived with us till she died. It was she who made this sharbath almost every Friday morning. Later it was my mother who made it. But we made it less and less often, as we grew up and homework and endless extra classes and tests took over, and my mother had less and less time, and we did not help her much either. Later, years after I was married and my husband and I moved to the US, I made sharbath for the very first time on my very own, mostly from some tips from my aged mother and from snippets of childhood memories.

I am a small child. It is Kolkata in the late 1960s. I would get in the way, trip my silver-haired grandmother up by getting entangled in her sari, but she would never shoo me away. The dusty raisins (that sometimes looked like those ugly pig ticks to me) were obsessively picked over, de-stemmed, washed thoroughly, and soaked in water in a stainless steel dish. Covered and left to soak in the corner of the kitchen. Like bread, it sat to brood, but instead of rising like a cloud, the raisins plumped up, turned as fat as the seven fat cows that good old Joseph the Dreamer saw in his vision. (As a child I thought Joseph was so handsome—at least, he was handsome on the cover of my Ladybird book). I hovered around the swelling raisins, peeking under the lid of the dish to report progress. I was waiting for the next step.

When I was a teenager, still dealing with the loss of my grandmother, I understood for the first time what caregivers of the aged and dying went through. I came face to face with death, the death of a loved one at home. And the rituals, (just simple ones as we weren't religious and did not know the prayers), the funeral, and the trauma of it all.

During the a year or so after my grandmother's death, I was probably depressed, though no one, including myself, knew it. When we made sharbath, I missed my grandma, and nothing gave me joy. Not even Friday sharbath. But some years later, something happened that lightened things up a little for me. And it had to do with raisins.

We were preparing for Yom Kippur, and we often prepped the raisins a few days in advance. About a half kilo of raisins and been meticulously picked over, washed, and drained by my mother. Then she had laid them out to dry, as she often did with rinsed vegetables and fruit, on a tea towel resting in a bamboo souk—a woven wicker tray in which rice (or grain) is threshed to remove chaff and stones. That day she placed a low stool in the bright sunlight that filled our gorgeous verandah, and she put the souk on it. She spread the dark damp gems out with her fingers to make sure they were in a single layer and would dry quickly.

A couple of hours later, the raisins had disappeared. We all came to look for them, amazed at this strange disappearance. It's the damn crows was the general consensus. The crows were always stealing things, always hanging about our windows. They got scraps from us all the time. Some of them we knew quite well. And now they were getting bolder. Perhaps it was a stray cat or two, or even a couple of those huge hairy rats—they could have sneaked in through the kitchen window in the afternoon when everyone was napping after lunch. Perhaps the window had been left ajar by mistake? Or the creatures had climbed through the railings of our second floor verandah in broad daylight?

The next morning we discovered that our dog, Goofy, was acting strange. He wobbled and weaved as he walked. Then he got "sick as a dog" indeed. No one had given him a thought. It would have been easy for him to stand on his hind legs, for his shaggy face to reach the raisins and swallow a souk-full of them in a few gulps. The puzzle was solved. The culprit? A gluttonous Silky Sidney terrier with a bellyful of fast-swelling raisins! The poor fellow threw up and defecated everywhere. I'll say no more. But we laughed and laughed. To this day we remember and laugh: deep belly laughs. And so that story ends.

Let's start again. With a fresh kilo of raisins. Cleaned and washed till they glisten. Then soaked. Then strained, put into a dekchi, covered with water and set to boil on the gas stove.

The raisins roll in their own juices in the darkening water. Then they simmer slowly till the froth rises up all frizzy and curly like my hair. Then Granny turns the stove off, takes the dekchi off the heat, covers it. Patting my hair, she says, "Let it cool." Agony. Wait, wait, wait. Was this what adult life was all about? A good lesson learned early.

Soon enough, it is time to strain the almost-purple liquid, smash the pulp and squeeze the last drops of juice out. And make sure no seeds escaped. Now, again, I think of the figure of Autumn in Keats' poem, slow and almost intoxicated with the fumes emanating from the apples being pressed. The juice oozing, her eyes drooping. Her mind lost in dreams. I become this sleepy, dreamy girl. When I open my eyes I can't see the people I knew. The scenes around me have changed too.

Draksha-cha sharbath. Raisin or kishmish sherbet. Or angoor ka ras. Or whatever it may be called in your community. Our homemade sharbath made from special grapes called sultanas. Dried grapes as long as the first section of your index finger, grapes with large pips that had originated in the Middle East and were brought to India by Afghani and Kashmiri merchants, who sold them to us in New Market. Long live the vineyards and long live the hands that grew these grapes, that protected them and tended them, that picked them and dried them, that endured endless hardships, the hands that brought them to our land, sometimes through dangerous and difficult terrain, through rocky paths and mountain passes, to our markets all over India.

Long live draksha-cha sharbath. Long live the hands prepared the sharbath. We poured the sharbath into small glasses—whiskey shot glasses from Scotland with each one bearing a pastoral scene, bought by my marine engineer father on one of his voyages. Kept pouring till the sharbath spilled over into the saucers below, to symbolize abundance, blessing. Like in King David's psalm. We said barakha together, drank from the exquisite glasses, and then from the saucer. This is our harvest I carry with me. My cup runneth over.

# Gourami Fish Tale

At twelve, I had only seen the "Kissing" kind
in the Mumbai aquarium, the platter-flat pink gouramis

with enormous lips sucking at each other's mouths
for an eternity till boredom made me look around

for something more shocking. But the edible kind
I never saw until Captain Da Silva happened to catch one

in Lake Powai, (where he invited
some sailor friends to fish), its brown-

black scales shining like melted chocolate, one white
spot bright near its gills and a line of tinier dots

trailing along its spine till they faded
into tail.  The men fished for carp, for tilapia,

but my little-girl-job was to snag bait—slippery
chilvas (that's what Captain Da Silva called

this minnow-like fish), and proud I grew
of my silver arrows darting about in the blue

plastic bucket. But I craved big game,
and tried the heavier tackle.  A sharp tug

at my slack line made me yell, ecstatic
as a shadow emerged—a gourami it was

(declared Captain Da Silva, and a good
size too)! Its sulky protruding lips gaped,

desperate, and I gasped in horror, and yet
joy fluttered like a hundred fins

in the ocean of my chest, while the fishing rod shivered
with the small weight of my prize, the dying fish

*46*

flipping and flapping on the rough boards
of the wooden machaan. Squeamish at first

to pull the barbed torment from its bloody
face, I got bolder, (won much praise

from all) for removing the hook
from the thick-lipped mouth that kissed

and kissed at the empty air, at the terrifying
churn of demon faces above it, and, gulped

the poison oxygen until my dad released it
into a yellow nylon-string net

which held the catch, quickly lowering it
into the water. Innocent babe of the lake,

frightened soul—pierced, tortured ,
suffocating slowly all the way home,

betrayed by me (this fierce savior
and lover of animals, this grand  Little Lady

of No Mercy), and fried crisp that night.
Eating two pieces

I am told (no mean feat for a girl
so young), removing the bones

with help from my mother, I chatter on
about how I caught it, while our friends

pat my back, chug Johnny Walker,
tell my dad I have his genes, this was no

small catch, a keeper indeed, (wink wink)
the envy of officers and anglers.

# Green Kaanji and Destiny

the house always smelled different
lighter, somehow fresher
fragrant in a way that it didn't
when red curries were cooked

hunks of ginger garlic onion smashed
and ground on the ridged stone
scooped into a steel bowl

then oil heated in a dekchi
(peanut oil Postman brand
when I was young) till it smoked
a handful of kari leaves
with one or two green chilis
seeds removed (we could not
deal with much heat)
thrown in

(ah, the crackling, the fragrance)
and the wet paste added soon after
what a sizzle
and splatter and noses and eyes
watering briefly
stirred on a medium flame
a slow stir stir stir
with a dash of cumin and turmeric
and a half-palmful of coriander powder
salt to taste

mouth-watering the smell
filling the rooms
wafting out the windows
attracting crows
to sit on the sill and caw

masala never browned
just gently fried
rawness cooked out

the spices mellowed
just till it passed the final
sniff test

and what could compliment
this green deliciousness

mild fish like paplet
(these pomfrets were cheap back then)
sometimes local chickens
tough birds stewed into softness
or a winter vegetable like kohlrabi
or cauliflower, peas with
the ubiquitous potato

what made this kaanji green
as a tropical pond
oh the *dhanya*, so *dhanya*—
a blessing and the blessed herb
bunches of cilantro leaves
mud-smeared coriander washed
picked clean of grit and earthworms
then ground on the same stone
with a splash of water

a cup of green shining liquid
poured in right at the end
finished with a quick boil
and a lavish squeeze of lime
(fingers still exuding the smell
of the rind as you ate)

emerald kaanji of the Konkan
my ancestors learned to cook
when these west coast villages
became home

so comforting (sometimes
with coconut milk
for a richer curry)
yet so feisty citrus

bursting on the tongue
the tang of cilantro

a dish I loved so much
that once as a young girl
I could not stop eating it

slurping the velvety goodness
into my mouth
gorging on tender cubes
of kolhrabi and butter-soft potatoes

until, alarmed, my mother
swept the dish off to the kitchen
(only I was left at the table
still cleaning my plate
with my fingers) and did
we both learn the truth that day

that this little girl
mouth full of green curry
skinny weak child
a poor and picky eater
(eyes bigger than her stomach)

(who could know what or who I would turn into
when I grew up  and who knew
what "foodie" meant
did the word even exist then)

had the makings of a glutton
was destined to be
obsessed with food

# Kaulee Haddi

Savory crunch of soft bone,
how good it tasted in curry,
kaulee haddi,

peninsular tip of breast bone
from a small desi chicken
dad bought on the pavement

at Pul bazaar. Mom grumbled as she picked
clotted sand from its thin tight skin
before she cooked it,

kept feet, gizzard for stock.
My father loves boki flesh,
tender breast meat steeped in flavor,

falling off the triangle
of translucent bone. The supple end
curves to a pliant tongue

drunk with masala—
ginger warm, garlic sharp,
coriander mellow. But he rarely

ate it, breaking off that kaulee tip
with his wiry engineer fingers
salty with memories

of sea, flecked with rice and curry,
so that even when we were grown,
and especially

when we returned to visit, he fed
my sister, or me the precious kaulee haddi.
His harsh words forgotten,

we watched him bend,
melt the hard beaten bones
of his tough maritime heart.

# Homegrown

—*Chicago*

My peppy chili plant
lives on my window sill.
Its parrot-green pods
spice many a curry
on summer night's so hot
that my clothes cling to my body
and I peel them off like skin.

Though bred here in temperate climes,
sheltered from the outside world—
it still knows it's autumn.
It's heart is as tropical as can be.

Branches thin and bony
reach out of a terracotta bowl,
drip brown and yellow leaves.
But strung like scarlet macaws
on a vine, are ripe chilies,
so alive, restless,
look ready for flight.

I harvest the bright fruit—
save them for the cruelest
of cold nights.
Then clip ragged edges
of the generous giver,
shush the rustling of the last
brittle leaves, and let it sleep.

Warm in its belly though winter,
it will wake just before spring.
Tiny tear-drop buds
burst into white flame
here and there on stems
as bright as tree snakes.

And for one more year,
it will burn its red fires
in my little kitchen,
sear my lonely tongue
with tropical passion.

# At the Edge of Park Circus

*—Kolkata*

**1.**

Evening fills with smoke as
chulahs are lit. Grey puffs rise.
Dogs bark.

        Women flap palm leaf fans,
        flames rise in the red clay
        stoves on pavements,
        enamel dishes clink

from under thatched roofs,
drying saris droop.
At home, our eyes
begin to itch and water.

**2.**

My mother coughs. Turning off the gas stove,
Mum pours the tea into the thermos,
fills my cup. We sit together, sip slowly.
I search the steel tins for a snack.

The vendor downstairs is roasting
peanuts in sand, I hear the shush-
shush in his loop-handled black kadhai.
Our neighbors across the street

light oil diyas, fold their palms,
pray. They carry burning incense –
sometimes jasmine or champa,
through every room in their flats. Bell

sounds drown in traffic. Today, though
the garbage smells are stronger,
I can tell it is sandalwood they're burning,
fumes spill through the air and through

the window. Mosquitoes ride the wave of dusk,
whine around our ears. We rush
to close the wooden shutters. This winter evening
the wind blows from the east. Smell the pavement-

fried foods,  small-shack parathas, rumali roti,
kababs, and the daily reek from Tangra's
tanneries. From the Oriya cook's
stall –wedged between Joy

pharmacy and Salim's car repair shop,
it's potato singaras and red- brown onion
pakoras— the chilies in his lentil batter
are pure heat. My tongue licks the breeze,

swallows the fire, hungers for a taste.
Peppery papads fry in mustard
oil by the climbing merciless flow of traffic,
at the corner of old Char number pul.

**3.**

How the broadened Char number

bridge arching over rail tracks

ruined

the quiet. Now dust from the deep

dug holes for the fly-over settles in each

morsel of the new New Park Street, where an auto-

rickshaw will smash the right femur of my father's ghost

crossing Bright street, where my girl-specter

waits

for the bus to take me to school –the tiffin

of mint-chutney sandwiches my mother

made tucked in my bag, where everyday

there is an accident when a vendor

shoots

across the road between traffic signals

to buy bread and a bhad of tea, and no child

plays cricket on the road,  no one can

cross

the flood

of buses, lorries, cars, motorbikes,

to buy singara and sandesh from Nabalok Sweet Shop.

**4.**

                the gentle face of my mother
                looks through the cracked glass

        of the window of our shut-down flat
      it is 2 a.m. and she knows my plane has landed

                and waits for the car to pull in
                (she's made tea it's in the thermos

                she's kept the biscuit dubba ready)
                I see her face is at the window

                she waves when she sees the car
                tires crunch broken glass and litter

                    I climb out jet-lagged
                    crumpled as a stale napkin
                    smiling up at her and weeping

        our eyes cling through the dusty glass
        our eyes cling through the dusty glass

smiling up at her and weeping
crumpled as a stale napkin
I climb out jet-lagged

tires crunch broken glass and litter
she waves when she sees the car

I see her face at the window
(she's kept the biscuit dubba ready

she's made tea it's in the thermos)
and waits for the car to pull in

it is 2 a.m. and she knows my plane has landed
the window of our shut-down flat

looks through the cracked glass
the gentle face of my mother

# Never Forget the Chironje

not the usual savory fried puris
flat and round and large
as the palm of your hand—

the ones we might eat
with rich mutton curry
on birthdays
or anniversaries

but the special ones
the high holiday ones

seven-layered ones if you
followed the rules
half-moon shaped confection
filled to the tightly pinched
or zig-zagged seam
with ghee-roasted semolina
coarse shredded coconut
chopped raisins and nuts
deep fried

in our big karahi
then laid out in steel thalis
to cool
sprinkled with powdered
sugar and the brown globes
of fat charoli nuts

who knew heaven could be like this
it was never enough to hang around
my mother and grandmother
while they worked
sweat beads on their foreheads
and tempers sharp

but it was my obsession to watch
and wrap myself
in the fragrance and to wait

they knew great secrets
I would never learn

oh I remember the crunch
when I bit into the first hot ones—
the trial ones the crooked or
the split-in-the-oil ones
those that never made it
to the table my face nearly
plastered to the plate

tasting what they asked me to taste
telling them what was lacking
sweet or salt, devouring
love-filled crumbs they gave me

and me thinking they were immortal
that there would never be
a time in our lives without
them or our khus-khusi karanje.

# Pantoum for Chik-cha Halwa

*—Halwa made for festivals and special occasions*

whose hands worked hard to make this halwa
whose hands soaked the mounds of wheat
how we waited three days and nights
how chik was extracted from grain

whose hands soaked the mounds of wheat
knew each step of the recipe
how to squeeze the chik from grain
to slowly boil the thick beads of juice

did they learn each step of the recipe
from a new culture from a new land
to slowly boil the thick beads of juice
did they miss loved ones left behind

from a new culture from a new land
did they taste their ancestors' food
did they miss loved ones left behind
those lost in the deluge shipwrecked

did their tongues taste their ancestors' food
was this so different from sweets of home
those lost in the deluge and wreck
would never come back to life

so very different from sweets of home
sugar coconut milk colored pink thickening
those lost in the deluge shipwrecked
would their spirits whisper old recipes

sugar rose-tinted coconut milk thickening
tired arms bated breath silky cubes cooling
do spirits whisper old recipes
in a new land new life new history

tired arms bated breath silky cubes cooling
sprinkled with poppy seed slivered nuts
new land new life new history
food and ways you made your own

sprinkled with poppy seed slivered nuts
how we waited how we waited
the food and ways you made your own
your hands working hard to make this halwa

# The Laadu Makers

Even before my eyes open, my mouth starts watering. The air vibrates with the smell of roasting besan and ghee. Oh my, my mother is making besan laadus today. Is it my birthday? Is it their anniversary? I roll over and sniff the air. But it's gone. Just like all the other fragrances.

My mother is young and beautiful. She has glowing skin, large eyes, well-defined eyebrows, and a big nose—a feature which I have inherited. She has very long hair, braided in a plait that reaches below her knees. I never saw her hair worn like this—it is how she wore it before I was born. I've seen photographs. And I've seen pictures of tables laid out for Shabbath prayers and dinner at her parents' home. The polished brass Star of David oil lamp, lace tablecloths, platters of fruit and small cups of raisin sharbath. Or am I imagining that room, that table? Did I imagine it all?

So much is fading already, but the tastes never do. Neither do the smells, the smiles or the sorrows. My body is the vault that holds these histories, these memories. They are mine and mine alone. No one else in our family will remember the same things or remember them the same way, even if they were present then, at the same time and place.

Her hands are quick as she stirs the dried channa—split chickpeas—in the tava. From a pale yellow, they turn to beige, to gold-brown. Then she grinds them by hand till they turn into a medium-fine powder. A few crunchy pieces remain. She adds this ground besan to a large flat-bottomed karahi where the ghee is already warmed and ready. Stir, stir, stir. She wipes her forehead with the edge of her Calico sari pallav. My grandmother has come to check if she is doing it right. Tough bossy woman who takes over my mother's life from the time she is married to my father.

It is time to shake in the sugar little by little. The greyish crystals are large and crunchy and not all of them melt completely. Stir, stir, stir. Slowly, it is all coming together. The aroma is thick and sweet and spreads all over the house, and wafts off the balcony to the other balconies and houses, and breezes blow it down the street. The crows hang around the kitchen window. Today they seem antsier than other days. So am I, as I wait for the rituals to be over. They will get their share too.

Now she adds the fried raisins and cashews into the almost-pliant, almost-sticking- to-the-pan mixture. Earlier that day, she has picked the raisins and cashews over for stones and they have been washed and air-dried. Still it is not unusual for a grain of sand to hide in a crevice somewhere and appear suddenly under your molar when you are eating. Ouch. The pleasure and the pain. Inseparable, sometimes.

Granny is inspecting the mixture with her fingers. It's time to taste. Yes!!! My turn now. *Have you washed your hands?* Yes, yes, yes. I drop a blob on my tongue. Yes, yes, it's so good. *Mmmm*, she says as she does the same. Now we all dig in with our hands. Not to eat, but to roll the sticky-crumbly mixture between our palms. We form lime-sized balls and lay them out on a tray to harden. Then we will arrange them in our big steel dubbas. Some we will distribute to our neighbors and friends. But the rest is ours. For now we keep rolling, rolling, rolling. How I long to lick my fingers as we do this! They are watching my every move, so I don't. The reward is exquisite, so I will wait patiently. I can handle the wait. I am grown up now. Or so I think.

I will wait for the laadu, the gold globe that is made by their hands. I will bow my head and open my palms to receive it. A world held in their hands, then placed in mine. Heavy and earthy in my palms. Its deep and nutty flavor coats my tongue as I stand here at the edge of reality. This is not a figment of my imagination. It's what makes it all real. That the joy existed. That my parents, Ruby and Sunny, existed, and my grandma Hannah, existed. That love wrapped around me like these aromas. That my mouth and tongue are blessed by them. Goud-goud bolah, they say in Maharashtra on the day they feed you a spiky little bead of sugar and sesame seeds. Speak only sweet words. The wise hearts of the laadu makers taught me—good thoughts, words and deeds. And what of contentment? They blessed me with that too. No matter how little or how much I may have or own, how my situation may change from year to year, I, laadu eater, bow humbly to the ones who made me who I am, who sacrificed and never asked for thanks, and whom I never celebrated enough. And I ask for their forgiveness, for all of those things, but most of all for not writing down their recipes, their magic words.

# Prophet of the Rock

*—It is believed that Prophet Elijah, on his journey to heaven in a fiery horse-drawn chariot, visited a place in near Karle village in Maharashtra,. Today, Ghodya-cha Tap, or the Elijah Rock, as it is popularly called, is a place of pilgrimage, and Malida ceremonies are held there to honor him.*

Wild prophet with fiery eyes like the sun
whom the ravens fed in the desert

for whom miracle bread appeared in Jordan
and jugs of water, it was not your time to go

but when it was a blazing orb appeared
drawn by magnificent horses

manes flowing hooves thundering
chariot wheels flaming

spinning spinning

it was your time wise sage
your reward came from the skies

alive you rose up in glory
climbed the clouds into the heavens

spinning spinning

as it is written
on your way you flew down to visit us

the village flared with light
your chariot landed upon rough rock

sparks and wonder filled the humid air
our ancestors saw your face

spewing fire hooves clashed on stone
wheels aflame

spinning spinning

we know you were here
the land speaks your name

Oh protector this is where
the mighty chariot wheels churned

spinning spinning

ripping through rock
a long jagged tear

and horses of fire whose hooves
struck the earth

cleft the rock
two hoof marks remained

deep prints deep memories
such wondrous signs you left

before flames shot up into the sky
you rose up to the sun

swept away to your destination
in a terrifying whirlwind again

spinning spinning

# A Chirota for My Thoughts

this fine flaky treat was often made
from left over chironji dough

rolled out in flat circles
ghee-smothered with fingers

piled on each other folded and rolled
folded and rolled again

full of hidden "puthers"—feathers
which fluffed up miraculously

as it rose up singing
out of hot oil

a crisp golden disc
delicate as eggshells

dusted with sugar or drizzled with a glaze
then studded with pistas and charoli

eaten so fast the fine sprays of crumbs
settled everywhere like dust

I pressed my little index finger
into it and sucked

or licked off the old dining table
with my tongue

some days paralyzed with lost-ness
and weak limbs I pretend

unhealed wounds and home fallen
to ruin are made whole

broken slivers I salvage
from inside those stainless steel tins

the indestructible dubbas we owned
etched with our names

# Once Upon a Shabbath

Every Friday I light candles,
say the words I was taught to say.

I hear my father bellow
the first few words of the prayer.
My mother's soft tones.
Once the wicks we lit
were in oil lamps set
in my grandmother's
wood and silver-embossed
Star of David on the wall.

We gather around the Formica-topped
dining table, wearing white kippahs
crocheted by my grandmother,
on our heads. Lift up our right hands,
palms held towards the light
of the just-lit candles.
Incense swirls like mist.

My grandmother is holding
her upturned palms in front of her,
bowing her head as though reading
a book when she prays.
Barukh ata Adonai Elohenu…we chime
together. Amen echoes
in the cramped, dusty room.
Tight hugs, loud Shabbath Shaloms.
We sweat in the stillness, then
turn the fan back on.
The candle flames sway
this way and that.

Clinging to my mother and father,
I do not let them go for a long while.
I am only visiting.
I am a stranger,
I will go far away,
again and again,

leaving them behind
in their old age.

Rarely do we make draksha-cha sharbath.
Remembrance of such sweetness
on the tongue. The barakha
for the juice of grapes.
But, we gather with old friends—
Johnny Walker, Old Monk,
say barakha over wine. Sip
Coca Cola, fresh lime juice.
Easy chatter. Feast of mutton curry
rich with crushed fried onions,
and basmati rice scented with bay leaves,
all made by my mother and Rabiya.
Rabiya, who learned to cook our
dishes better than she could cook her own.
Old and bowed as she was, she
climbed the two flights of steep
stairs, wailing, when my mother died.
I have lost her, too. She who wept
and told me not to go to America.
She who for years made our daily meals,
our special dishes for weekends.
Flattened, pan-fried bombil,
or pomfret, potatoes golden-
crisp at the edges.

Sometimes, my siblings are visiting,
one from the same city, one from another.
Sometimes, spouses and children too.
How many times were we all together?
I can count on the fingers of just one hand.
Our paths diverged so very long ago.

Friday evening.
The patriarch beaming.
He who dreamed his tribe
would congregate around him,
children would live close by,
grandchildren adore him.

Who could predict the wrath
of fate, disappointments,
heartache?

One night suddenly, my mother leaves us.
Her tired heart gives out.
Two years later, my father's lungs
collapse. I am adrift
in darkness. Years of silence
between estranged siblings.
Rarely together, except in shards
of unreliable memory, photographs.
Now WhatsApp carries
hellos, Shabbath Shalom,
across the oceans. Shared
news here and there. Brief visits.

It is Friday. A vermillion
and mauve Michigan sunset.
My partner is by my side.
At my dining table stand
my mother and father, faces lit up.
Behind them, ancestors shimmer.
As I light my tea lights, blue
flames glow in azure bowls.
I raise my palm in prayer,
say the words
they taught me to say.

My beloveds are with me.
That is blessing enough.

# Notes

## A Chirota for Your Thoughts and Never Forget the Chironji:

In Marathi the chironji is also called karanji. The plural form is chironje and karanje. The same rule applies to chirota and chirote.

## Choral Sonnet:

DNA tests of the Bene Israel over a period of four years were studied by Dr. Tudor Parfitt, Jewish Studies Professor as the London School of Oriental and African Studies and geneticist Dr. Neil Bradman. The study found that DNA contained the Cohenim gene, which is traced back to Aaron, the brother of Moses, who began the hereditary Israelite priesthood. More information at:

*https://timesofindia.indiatimes.com/city/mumbai/geneticist-helps-mumbai-jews-reinforce-sense-of-identity/articleshow/29493656.cms*

*https://timesofindia.indiatimes.com/indias-children-of-israel-find-their-roots/articleshow/16588182.cms*

*Efrati, Ido, "Study Finds Genetic Connection Between Indian Bene Israel and Middle Eastern Jews", Haaretz, April 11, 2016: https://www.haaretz.com/jewish/2016-04-11/ty-article/.premium/genetic-connection-found-between-bene-israel-and-mideast-jews/0000017f-f670-d5bd-a17f-f67ab4c80000*

## Kaulee Haddi:

Marathi for soft or tender bone.

## Not One Fish:

Marathi names of fish:
Bangda—Mackarel
Paplet—Pomfret
Tarli—Sardine
Information about David Ezekiel Rahabi:

*https://www.britannica.com/topic/Cochin-Jews#ref1173196*

*https://www.britannica.com/topic/Bene-Israel#ref222427*

## The Laadu Makers:

Laadu: In Marathi the word is pronounced laa-doo. In Hindi it's pronounced ludd-oo.

**The Significance of Prophet Elijah:**

Elijah, the prophet, the shaman, the fiery servant of God of Abraham, is very dear to the Bene Israel, and it is believed that his chariot of fire drawn by horses of fire departed from the heavens from a particular rock in Southeast Maharashtra. This is an important place of pilgrimage where Malida ceremonies are held. Elijah is honored in all kinds of thanksgiving celebrations.

**Current Populations:**

The descendants of the Bene Israel have thrived in India and around the world. The estimated population in India today is about 3,500, and their global population is about 95,000.

**Sources:**

*The Jews of India* by Benjamin J. Israel (Mosiac Books)

*The Bene Israel of India: Some Studies* by Benjamin J. Israel (Orient Longman)

*India's Jewish Heritage, Ritual, Art, and Life Cycle* by Shalva Weil (Marg Publications)

**Further Reading:**

*Bene Appetit: The Cuisine of Indian Jews* by Esther David (HarperCollins)

*Growing up Jewish in India,* edited by Ori Z Soltes (Niyogi Books)

*The Guide to the Bene Israel of India—Culture, History and Customs* by Eliaz Reuben-Dandeker (Kammodan Mocadem Publishing House)

*The History of the Bene Israel* by Haeem Samuel Kehimkar

*India's Bene Israel: A Comprehensive Inquiry and Sourcebook* by Shirley Berry Isenberg (Judah L. Magnus Museum)

*Jewish Communities of India: Identity in a Colonial Era* by Joan G. Roland (Routledge)

*Jews, Judaizing Movements and the Traditions of Israelite Descent in South Asia* by Navras Jaat Aafreedi (Pragati Publications)

*Songs of Translation: Bene Israel Performance from India to Israel* by Anna Schulz (forthcoming from Oxford University Press)

*Studies of Indian Jewish Ancestry* by Nathan Katz (Manohar Publishers)

*Who Are the Jews of India?* by Nathan Katz (University of California)

# About the Author

**Zilka Joseph** is the author of five collections of poetry. Her work is influenced by Indian and Western cultures, and her Bene Israel roots. Her poems have appeared in journals such as *Poetry, Poetry Daily, Kenyon Review Online, Michigan Quarterly Review, Rattle, Asia Literary Review, Punch Magazine, The Bombay Literary Magazine,* and in anthologies like *101 Jewish Poems for the Third Millennium, Home: Michigan State University & Short Edition, Kali Project, RESPECT: An Anthology of Detroit Music Poetry, Yearbook of Indian Poetry in English, Converse: Contemporary Indian Poetry in English. The Dictionary of Midwestern Literature* and *The Routledge Encyclopedia of Indian Writing in English* include her contributions.

*Lands I Live In* and *What Dread* were nominated for PEN and Pushcart awards. *Sharp Blue Search of Flame* (Wayne State University Press) was a Foreword INDIES Award finalist, and *Sparrows and Dust* was a Notable Best Indie Award winner and a Notable Asian American Poetry Book. *In Our Beautiful Bones* was also a Foreword INDIES Award finalist, and was nominated for PEN, Pushcart, Griffin and American Book awards. Joseph received a Zell Fellowship, the Michael R. Gutterman Award for poetry, and the Elsie Choy Lee Scholarship from the University of Michigan. She teaches creative writing workshops and is a manuscript advisor and mentor to writers in her community.

Joseph was born in Mumbai, lived in Kolkata, and now lives in Ann Arbor, Michigan, USA.

*www.zilkajoseph.com*

# About the Cover Artist

Born Raina Rahael Ezekiel into Parsi and Bene Israel families, in Bombay, India, Raina Imig grew up in Europe and India. She is a lifelong student of the Integral Yoga of Sri Aurobindo and The Mother.

An artist and teacher, she lives in Portland, Oregon. She is honored to serve her community, both in person locally as well as virtually worldwide, as a Shamanic practitioner and energy healer.

*https://shamandalaservices.wordpress.com*

# Recent Titles from Mayapple Press...

David Michael Nixon, *A Wolf Comes to My Window,* 2024
               Paper, 40pp, $15.95
               ISBN: 978-1-952781-22-3
Zilka Joseph, *Sweet Melida,* 2024
               Paper, 60pp, $19.95
               ISBN: 978-1-952781-19-3
Eleanor Lerman, *Slim Blue Universe,* 2024
               Paper, 68pp, $20.95
               ISBN: 978-1-982781-17-9
Cati Porter, *Small Mammals,* 2023
               Paper, 78pp, $19.94 plus s&h
               ISBN 978-1-952781-15-5
Eleanor Lerman, *The Game Cafe,* 2022
               Paper, 160pp, $22.95 plus s&h
               ISBN 978-1-952781-13-1
Goria Nixon-John, *The Dark Safekeeping,* 2022
               Paper, 92pp, $19.85 plus s&h
               ISBN: 978-1-952781-11-7
Nancy Takacs, *Dearest Water,* 2022
               Paper, 84pp, $19.95 plus s&h
               ISBN: 978-1-952781-09-4
Zilka Joseph, *In Our Beautiful Bones,* 2021
               Paper, 108pp, $19.95 plus s&h
               ISBN: 9780-1-952781-07-0
Ricardo Jesús Mejías Hernández, tr. Don Cellini,
*Libro de Percances / Book of Mishaps,* 2021
               Paper, 56pp, $18.95 plus s&h
               ISBN: 978-952781-05-6
Eleanor Lerman, *Watkins Glen,* 2021
               Paper, 218pp, $22.95 plus s&h
               ISBN: 978-1-952781-01-8
Betsy Johnson, *when animals are animals,* 2021
               Paper, 58pp, $17.95 plus s&h
               ISBN: 978-1-952781-02-5
Jennifer Anne Moses, *The Man Who Loved His Wife,* 2021
               Paper, 172pp, $20.95 plus s&h
               ISBN: 978-1-936419-96-8

For a complete catalog of Mayapple Press publications, please visit our website at *mayapplepress.com.* Books can be ordered direct from our website with secure on-line payment using PayPal, or by mail (check or money order). Or order through your local bookseller.